Top Tips fo

Over 300 Top Tips and Handy Hints
for Canoe and Kayak Coaches

Plas y Brenin Canoe Department

Pesda Press - Wales

www.pesdapress.com

Published in Great Britain 2002
Reprinted 2004

by Pesda Press
'Elidir'
Ffordd Llanllechid
Rachub
Bangor
Gwynedd
LL57 3EE

ISBN   0-9531956-6-X

Printed in Great Britain by Cambrian Printers - Wales

Introduction

You cannot learn to paddle a canoe or kayak in the UK without being influenced by 'The Brenin' and its canoe department, be it first-hand, on our courses, or indirectly, via one of the thousands of coaches or paddlers we have helped to train over the last 30 years.

Our coaches have been at the forefront of the sport's development and the massive developments in coaching and leadership skills during this period. It makes sense to print a simple, no nonsense book of ideas from the department's coaches. Some of the ideas they will have thought up themselves and some they will have collected as 'coaching shareware' by watching other coaches. The simplicity of the ideas belies the combined experience and breadth of expertise of the contributors that helps to make this the best £4-95 any aspiring coach could spend.

We would like to acknowledge the contributions and influence of the many coaches who have been involved in the development of canoeing and kayaking at Plas y Brenin and have directly or indirectly contributed to this book.

Loel Collins - Head of Canoe Department

Plas y Brenin Canoe Department

Contacts

Plas y Brenin,
National Mountain Centre,
Capel Curig,
Conwy,
LL24 0ET

Telephone: 01690-720214
Fax: 01690-720394
E mail: info@pyb.co.uk

Visit our website at: www.pyb.co.uk

Using This Book

Many readers will have already come across the analogy of the 'coach's toolbox'. The idea being that a coach has to collect lots of tools to aid his or her coaching. These may be aids to observations, exercises, games, similes, analogies and so on. The more experienced coach will have a different tool for almost every situation and type of learner. Some will be favourites that are used often and some will be hidden away, almost forgotten.

Some coaches' brains are like a 'tool bag'; all their tools are dumped in the same bag and they just rummage around till they find a suitable one. Some coaches have very organised 'toolboxes' with natty little compartments, neatly labelled in their mind's eye. The problem is that each coach will organise his or her 'toolbox' in a different way.

To that end no attempt has been made to organise this collection of 'tools' in a logical order. It is important that readers browse through them, select the ones they think they might find useful, experiment with their use, customise them to suit their needs and style, and then put them in the appropriate compartment of their own 'toolbox'.

Read on!

Plas y Brenin Canoe Department

1. Watch other coaches work and use their ideas. (It's not stealing, think of coaching tools as 'shareware').

2. When you admire someone's new paddle and buy the same model, you will probably need to buy one that is a different length and maybe even alter the feather to adjust it to your style and physique. Coaching tools are just the same; if you see a good ploy being used, you will need to experiment with it and subtly alter it so that it works for you.

3.   Whether on the sea or on a river, the more worried you are about real hazards the less able you are to concentrate on effective coaching.

4.   Whether on the sea or on a river, the more worried your students are about real hazards the less able they are to concentrate on effective learning.

5.   Try and find venues where the technical difficulty is high but the consequences are not serious.

6. When teaching complex paddle stroke sequences, get the student to use slightly shorter, lighter paddles to aid the development of the complex actions.

7. When teaching white water canoeing or kayaking, think of everything in terms of speed and angle.

8. Encourage students to look at least 3-4 boat lengths ahead of their actual position. This improves posture and anticipation skills.

9. To encourage a more open, extended paddling style in kayak, get students to imagine that they are holding a beach ball wedged between the paddle loom and the front of their buoyancy aid.

10. Alternatively get the student to imagine that their arms, paddle and body form a box shape which should be maintained when paddling. (Don't be religious about the box!)

11. When teaching bow rudders, try it first without a paddle. Get your students to gain forward speed and initiate the turn using their hands as paddles, then put their hands together side by side so that the palms of their hands form one 'blade' when the time comes to 'plant' the bow rudder. This encourages the forward lean and an appreciation of the subtle blade angle required.

12. When developing edge control, try getting your students to place a hand on their head, the other on their belly and dancing the salsa with their hips. Then swop the hands over and repeat.

13. As the coach, observe your paddlers in terms of the 5 B's: Body, Boat, Blade, Brain and Background.

14. When coaching anyone other than a complete beginner, you need to know what their current level of ability is. Don't take their word for it. Develop a range of exercises and games that can be used as a 'diagnostic tool'. 10 minutes structured observation will set you up for the rest of the day.

15.   A good diagnostic exercise is 'sea trials'. In a relatively sheltered bay, get your students to compare how their kayak behaves when paddling: down wind, upwind, across the wind, with the wind 30 degrees off the bow and with wind at 30 degrees off the stern. This does 3 things: it enables you to observe and analyse their boat handling skills, it enables them to familiarise themselves with the boats, and it gently warms them up.

16.   When accurate observation is important, use 'marks' on the bank or shore, on the boat and on the paddler.

17.   If there aren't enough marks already available, make your own. As an example, use electrical tape on the deck or the gunwale to make a series of marks that will enable you to quantify exactly how far forward the paddle is entering the water.

18. Key points to use as marks on the body are the centre-line of the torso, the face and the joints (shoulders, elbows, wrists).

19. Shapes can be useful when observing. Does the shape the boat carves through the water during a manoeuvre resemble a letter 'C', or is it more a 'J', or an 'L'?

20. Teach your students how to observe.

21. Spend time developing your students' understanding of their body's movement and actions within their boat, not just paddle movements.

22. Spend time developing co-ordinated movements as part of your warm-up with your students.

23.   Spend time ensuring that the equipment (all of it) is the correct size for your student.

24.   Use paddle wax on the paddle shaft to reduce the need for your clients to over grip the paddle. This reduces Repetitive Strain Injuries, reduces tiredness and improves feedback on subtle blade control.

25. Consider everything in terms of Balance, Accuracy and Timing. (BAT)

26. Use video feedback with visual learners.

27. Use demonstration as part of your feedback with visual learners.

28. Make the last 5 words of your verbal instruction the important ones.

29. When observing, if you spot a problem wait to see if it appears on the second run before you decide how to address it. Make sure it is a real problem rather than a 'one off'.

30. If you see a different problem on the second run, ask yourself if they have the same cause? If so, address that.

31.   The skills of coaching are generic.

32.   You coach people, not canoeing. Address the person's needs first.

33.   If you set an exercise and your student is upside down more than twice, the exercise is too hard and needs to be changed.

34.   If your student's performance suddenly drops, call time out.

35.   Coaching complex skill is like eating an elephant, best done in small bites over a long period.

36.   Don't bother teaching sculling for support.

37. When coaching canoe paddling, remember that the corrective element of the strokes is subtle, just like seasoning your supper.

38. Vary the environment within your practice sessions.

39. Make all your practice sessions bi-lateral.

40. Variety is the spice of practice!

41. Change angle, change speed, change edge, change side, change stroke combinations, change location. VARIATION - VARIATION - VARIATION!

42. Canoeing is a 'doing' sport. Simple formula for improving your coaching:
ACTION - PRACTICE - VARIATION!

43. Get your students to paddle with their eyes shut to improve their personal feedback.

44. If you can get your students to paddle with their eyes shut the environment is about right.

45. If they won't, ask yourself if the site is too hard!

46. If it's not, is the exercise too hard?

47. When encouraging edge control, get the students to physically lift the edge with their hand. This keeps the body upright and edge up.

48. Be passionate about your paddling.

49. 'Practice makes permanent' NOT 'Practice makes perfect'. (Dave Collins)

50. 'Perfect practice makes perfect'. (John Fazey)

51. You're valued for the quality of your feedback NOT the quantity.

52. Try telling your students to practise something 3 times, and do not provide feedback until they have finished.

53. For feedback to be effective the student should have time to absorb the information they are receiving from their senses. Try waiting until your student makes eye contact before you offer any feedback.

54. The coach can observe a great deal, but only the paddler can feel what is happening. When your student finishes the exercise and makes eye contact, try pausing so as to give time for the student to feedback to the coach. Sometimes they do all the work for you!

55. To get the most value from feedback, a student should repeat the performance within 30 seconds of receiving it ...so keep it brief!

56. A formula for vastly improved coaching performance: more visual feedback, more kinaesthetic feedback, much less audio feedback.

57. When coaching surfing, it is almost impossible to provide immediate feedback. You will need to develop your reviewing skills and use visualisation.

58. One way of providing sensory feedback during reviews of wave runs is to use a 'sand dune simulator'. After explaining what they should do on the next run, simulate the actions to be used in the run with your student sat in the kayak on the face of a sand dune.

59. Coach what you DO ...not what you THINK you do.

60. Ask your students! They will want to be involved.

61. By all means communicate with other coaches in jargon; talk with your students in English!

62. Never be afraid of going back to the foundation skills, these form the basis of all effective paddling.

63. Coach the foundation skills with the same passion you teach the technical stuff. If you do, your students won't mind revisiting the basics.

64. Spend time in other kinds of craft. If you kayak, paddle a canoe for a while. If you canoe, paddle a kayak for a while! If you do both try a wave-ski!

65. Spend as much time developing your coaching skills as your paddling skills.

66. If your students don't understand, it's your problem.

Plas y Brenin Canoe Department

67. Paddle because you love it.

68. Coach because you love it.

69.   Teach concepts and principles at the earliest opportunity.

70.   Think before you give your feedback.

71.   If you have a student in a brand new kayak, you will probably need to move the seat forwards to get the trim right.

72. For your students' sake, let them know if the kit isn't helping.

73. Good paddles are worth the money ...you can't fillet a fish with a chain saw!

74. If your students are bored, you're boring.

75.   When teaching new tandem crews, spend 30 minutes developing communication, co-ordination and co-operation skills, before you do the paddle stuff.

76.   When teaching edge control: edge at low speeds (knee, hip and buttock) - lean at high speeds (upper body).

77. When teaching the use of subtle weight shifts for gentle edging, get your students to imagine a painful boil on one of their buttocks. They will instinctively shift their weight onto the other one.

78. If a student is struggling with the concept of lifting and locking a knee to keep the boat edged, press down on the knee concerned and get them to resist the pressure. They will then know which muscles are involved and how it feels.

79. The controlling hand presents the paddle blade to the water, the hand closest to the wetted blade does the fine control, i.e. both hands are used to control the blade!

80. Paddle in your own time, when you're not coaching, for fun!

81. When teaching lining, pick a site with a good flow.

82. When teaching poling, start with a kneeling half pole and work up to standing stance and full pole.

83. When leading or coaching leadership, consider your role in terms of the following principles: communication, line of sight, tactical positioning and prevention is better than cure.

84. Read: White Water Safety and Rescue, Franco Ferrero ISBN 0-9531956-0-0

85. Leadership - Use common sense signals, i.e. ones that hardly need explanation, e.g. stop, come down, go that way. If you need any other signals, brief your group as you need to use them.

86. Leadership - No signal means no move.

87. Leadership - If one person in your group is feeling cold, scared or nervous, then the whole group are!

88.   If you ask for feedback, accept it graciously.

89.   Ask for feedback.

90.   If you ask questions, be prepared for a variety of responses.

91. If you want to train coaches, you MUST be able to work at the level they do.

92. The most important coaches are the ones working at an introductory level; don't ever forget that.

93. If you're feeling cold, scared or nervous get off the water.

94. Mathew Pincent's coach can't row faster than he can, but then he's not doing it on grade 3 white water. You don't have to be better than your students, but you must be safe!

95. Confidence comes from understanding, technique and practice because these lead to skilful performance. Not simply doing it lots!

96. True experts have a broad foundation of skills. Seek to coach people to be experts.

97. Get your clients to count the number of strokes it takes to complete a given manoeuvre; then try to reduce the number of strokes.

98.   SMILE!

99.   Get your students to smile. It's hard to be tense when you're smiling.

100. If a paddler is tense, any movement of the head is transmitted to the boat. The boat wobbles and the student gets more tense ...a downward spiral that ends in a capsize. Get your students to think of their abdominal muscles as a shock absorber. If they are feeling 'tippy' get them to imagine they are floppy rag dolls.

101. Structure your feedback.

102. When teaching the fundamentals of turning in white water the ends of the boats must be out of the water. This applies to turning in waves mid current and spinning in stoppers.

103. It also applies to turning in waves on the sea.

104. If your client is leaning in stoppers rather than edging, have them apply a bit of speed to achieve success, then reduce the speed to develop edge control.

105. Is the roll failing at the end of the stroke? Get them to cock the wrist of the upper hand towards the shoulder.

106. Is the roll failing because the body comes up early? Get them to nod their head towards the working paddle when they want to move their hips.

107. Is the roll failing because the head comes up early? Get them to look at the surface of the water as they roll up.

108. When teaching throw line skills, improve accuracy by having your students visualise a funnel, which they are throwing the line down.

109. When teaching throw line skills, improve accuracy by timing the release from the throwing hand so that it frames the casualty.

110. On balance, white water paddling protective equipment will assist an injured paddler so think twice about removing it!

111. Your first demonstration will present the overall form of the movement. A second demo will have a little effect as the form is now firmly fixed in your student's mind ...so make the first one a good one!

112. A paddle feather of 90 degrees is too much; a natural feather, if you need it, is somewhere between 45 and 60 degrees.

113. Use an asymmetric paddle in preference to symmetric blades.

114. Encourage paddlers to hold the paddle with a relaxed grip.

115. If your student has difficulty understanding the positioning of the paddle relative to the boat ask them to imagine they are sitting in the middle of a pizza that has been cut into quarters. (Kevin Danforth)

116. When teaching traditional canoe paddling strokes, encourage the paddler to move their top hand around on the palm grip to reduce the twist required from the wrist.

117. If your student has problems understanding the angle that the boat is relative to the water, ask them to imagine the flow of the current is running 12 to 6 on a clock face. You can then get them to set the boat to the correct time!

118. When breaking in and out, get your paddler to visualise opening a door.

119. If your students have difficulty understanding the position of the blade relative to the boat get them to visualise a clock face with the paddler in the centre. (12 dead ahead, 6 dead behind)

120. In windy conditions have your students paddle with their eyes shut and the wind on their faces, to try and set the angle to the wind.

121. Warm up your students both physically and mentally prior to the session.

122. When rolling or teaching 3D freestyle moves, students will struggle with understanding the immediate environment and their position in it. Do some 3D exercises on the bank to assist this, cartwheels, forward rolls, roly-polies, anything that requires movement and inverts!

123. When coaching 3D, don't let your student practise what they think the action is unless it's in the context of the move, i.e. if the movement is upside down or vertical, practise the move whilst upside down or vertical.

124. Use video coaching a lot when coaching rolling.

125. Video works best for you if you use it as part of your normal observation, and analyse it with your student.

126. Use a digital camera with a 3 or 4-inch playback screen.

127. Take 10 mins to work out how the video records and plays back.

128. Strokes that require the boat to be moving to work require subtle blade control to be effective ...rudder strokes in particular. Look out for excessive loss of speed as an indication that paddle movement is excessive.

129. Turns that use a brace are often made to work by excessive use of the brace so that it is in effect a reverse sweep. Look out for excessive loss of speed in a turn that finishes as a spin on the spot.

130. A good indicator of speed is the movement of the head relative to the background.

131. Another good indicator of speed being lost during a turn is the reduction in radius of the turn.

132. To a degree some speed can be regained by turning a bow rudder into a forward power stroke. The same effect can be created by not using a low brace at all and simply holding the paddle ready to provide a forward power stoke.

133. "There is nothing, absolutely nothing, half so much worth doing as simply messing about in boats."

Ratty – from The Wind in the Willows

by Kenneth Graham.

134. On a river rescue remember: paddler, boat, paddles - in that order.

135. In open water: boat, paddler, paddle - in that order.

136. "There is no try. Only do or do not. If you try you will fail" – Yoda, Star Wars

137. "Remember, there is no spoon." – see the film 'The Matrix'.

138. Duct Tape: Have lots!

139. Electricians tape, have lots!

140. Anyone who is scared of kayaking had a bad teacher.

141. There is a difference between river right and wave right. Work it out!

142. It's essential for your clients to understand that just because they stop paddling it doesn't mean the river has stopped.

143. You can't shout across a noisy river.

144. Ask your clients to question you, you'll learn more and they'll learn more.

145. Don't do what you've always done, you won't be learning anything!

146. The forward stroke is the most vital and the most neglected.

147. Forward paddling can be effectively coached while on a journey using a 'drip feed' method. Get your students to focus on one aspect of the paddling cycle for 10 minutes, then on a different aspect for the next 10 minutes and so on. After an hour, review the key points and then get them to try and bring them all together for the remainder of the journey.

148. If at the end of a sweep stroke you notice the elbow of the working arm bending up, check for effective trunk rotation.

149. If at the end of a sweep stroke you notice the elbow of the non-working arm bending up, check for a wider paddle stance.

150. Asking your client to look where they want to go can help but watch out for looking out of the corner of their eyes! Try asking them to face the direction in which they want to go.

151. Better still ask them to turn their head and shoulders to face the direction in which they want to go. This 'pre-rotation' not only focuses the mind on the target but also helps set the edge and turn the boat.

152. Your client's head will be tilted away from the edge you want lifted!

153. There is no such thing as a 'correct' paddle stroke, simply a variation that is the most appropriate version for the unique environment the paddler is in.

154. Most of paddlers' problems are due to poor posture. Poor posture prevents rotation which prevents effective strokes.

155. When watching a paddler, look from the side, the front, the back and the other side.

156. Clean rope: no knots, use hitches, you don't need a handle in your end of the throw line, less chance of a snag.

157. When teaching entrapment drills, do the first drill in slow time, try the second in silence after a planning session, and finally, try one with everyone holding their breath.

158. Contrary to popular belief, most people learn to paddle from their mates, your relationship with your student is very, very important.

159. When teaching rolling, to prevent overextension of the upper arm, put a tennis ball in the upper armpit and ask the student to keep it there during the roll.

160. When coaching canoe skills, always teach how to trim the boat before trying to do anything else.

161. When teaching white water technique, focus on hydrology and foundation skills before 'white water skills'.

162. Avoid referring to flat-water techniques as basic; try to use the term foundation skills, this is what they are.

163. For long-term retention of skills we need to teach the principle of good technique, not simply get the client to copy us.

164. Every coach should understand the learning process, how different people learn a physical skill.

165. At some point you need to just go boating, I mean for a month or two at the least.

166. At some point your students will simply need to go boating.

167. Be a paddler first, coach second, BCU coach last!

168. Men, on the whole are monophasic, can do one thing at a time.

169. Women are polyphasic, can do many things simultaneously.

170. When watching a demonstration a male student is likely to focus his observation on primarily the paddler and secondly their position on the water.

171. When watching a demonstration, a female student is likely to focus her observation on primarily the paddler's position on the water and secondly their paddle actions.

172. When observing a paddler, remember that you will see the result, not the cause, of a problem.

173. For most beginners, a paddle provides too much power. Start coaching balance and edging without it.

174. A paddle is not complicated, it's a stick with two big hands on it ...use it to pull you wherever you want to go.

175. Kayakers, learn from canoeists. When you've mastered a manoeuvre, try limiting yourself to one blade.

176. Use the quiet moments to hone foundation skills.

177. 'Play with purpose.' If you have a target or outcome (however trivial) in mind, you can compare your performance.

178. Beginners – if you're off in circles, try looking and aiming at a target, keep aiming at it and keep going until you get there.

179. Practise getting things right, don't practise giving up.

180. Practise getting things right, then practise correcting your mistakes – they will happen.

181. You can only improve if you admit there is room for improvement – especially under assessment.

182. Put an orange in the bottom of the boat – roll it forward, back, left or right to trim the hull.

183. Put a bottle in the bottom of the boat, and it will only roll left or right.

Plas y Brenin Canoe Department

184. Edge a kayak gently – it should be like turning up a knob, not flicking a switch.

185. Except when you need to edge it quickly! (usually as the result of a mistake!)

186. Edging into moving water is like jumping onto a moving bus – once you're there you can relax and go with the flow.

187. Assessment is not an end goal - it's a stepping stone!

188. Many students do the right things at the wrong time – make them point out the eddies and waves etc. – you already know where they are!

189. Sing the song of the river – fast or slow – loud or gentle – calm or staccatto – to match your paddling.

190. The river is heading downhill fast enough – only paddle downriver if you need even more speed.

191. To enter an eddy, or work across the current, you must do all the work.

192. Don't try to 'just make' an eddy – try to get right in the back of it.

193. To understand edging and trim – stick your hand out of the window of a car whilst travelling at speed.

194. Learning to cope with low brace turns is like riding a bike with stabilisers – better to keep paddling/pedalling.

195. Your paddle is designed to work well in water
 – keep it there – it doesn't work nearly as well in
 fresh air!

196. Don't pull too hard on the paddle, imagine the loom
 is a glass tube.

197. Don't squeeze the shaft too tightly, imagine it's a
 prize banana and you don't want to bruise it.

198. Never forget the 'three C's': chill, chill and chill.

199. Think of breaking in as throwing a stone across the river, it's a combination of speed and angle. Try it.

200. To understand speed and angle, get your students to throw a stone down the line of attack.

201. Paddling really hard in the wrong direction will only make things worse.

202. With students who have too much power and too little skill, get them to paddle at half speed and concentrate on accuracy for a while.

203. Learning bow rudders - Get your students to raft up in pairs facing each other. Then get them to try to squeeze the bow of their partners' boat out from between their boat and paddle. They won't be able to, but their muscles will experience the same resistance that they will feel when performing a bow rudder in moving water.

204. Learning bow rudders – Try setting your paddler up in the eddy and then pushing them into the current at the required speed and angle. They get to 'feel' what the end result should feel like without the overload of timing the strokes.

205. Pumping bow rudders is like stirring porridge. Keep your blade in the water and stir your way right round the pot.

206. Find out how far a full sweep stroke will turn your kayak. Now ask yourself, "How often do I need to do that?" Develop subtlety in your strokes.

207. Find out your students' hobbies, do they ski, surf, ride a bike, etc? Can they use these experiences to relate to paddling?

208. Starting with zero for a horizontal boat, give the degree of edge a score from 0 to 5 …6 is a capsize.

209. To sit on an edge of 1 or 2, imagine sharing a bar stool with someone – all your weight is on one buttock.

210. Get your students to call out the edge as they paddle. What they think may often be different to what you see.

211. Many paddling manoeuvres are concerned with angles of attack to the wind or the current. Try using a chinograph pencil and waterproof paper to draw diagrams for your students, or draw in the sand on the beach or the riverside.

212. Freestyle and surfing involves a 3D approach. Try making models of the wave with sand or mud and using a model of a paddler with bendy arms and torso to illustrate moves.

213. Surf, freestyle and white water paddling all require changes of pace and tempo. Get your students to paddle to imaginary music. Try 'the Blue Danube' for a nice sedate paddle followed by some 'Heavy Metal Thrash' for that 'must make' eddy.

214. Sometimes people need to paddle in a relaxed fluid fashion and other times they need to be really aggressive. Get your students to "paddle like a ballet dancer", and then for contrast, "paddle like a boxer". Pick your own characters.

215. A little fear is stimulating, a lot of fear makes you freeze or at the very least inhibits performance.

216. When dealing with fear, labels can make a big psychological difference. If there is something a student knows they can do but find frightening, try getting them to re-label it as exciting.

217. When choosing a line and whether to run it, your students should consider all the factors including the hazards. Once they make the decision to run it they must FOCUS on where they want to be and forget about the hazards. They've already decided that they have the skill to avoid them.

218. If you think about where you don't want to be ...that's exactly where you'll end up!

219. Get students to exaggerate their actions by getting them to 'demonstrate the skill to the others and make it really obvious'.

220. Don't kid yourself that a student has understood a new skill until you've seen them perform it several times, in several different situations.

221. Just because someone hasn't done loads of paddling, doesn't mean they are stupid.

222. Don't get annoyed with incompetent students. The whole point is that they don't know what they're doing ...they wouldn't be there otherwise.

223. There is no such thing as a stupid question only a stupid answer ...watch out!

224. "Work should absorb you, like an absorbing game. If it doesn't absorb you, if it's never any fun, don't do it." D H Lawrence

225. Break a goal into several achievable steps. Even if your students don't reach the end, they can still measure their progress.

226. When teaching trim and edge in an open canoe, place a couple of golf balls in the boat so the student can see the effect of trimming the boat more easily.

227. When introducing edge control, place a golf ball in the cockpit of the kayak so that it rolls from side to side. The student can feel and hear it.

228. Let other coaches watch you work and then ask them for feedback.

229. If you can't find a coach, find a video camera and coach yourself.

230. A good Goal is PURE: Positive, Understandable, Relevant, allows for the Environment.

231. As a general rule, stick to positive feedback. You want to leave your students with an image of what they are trying to achieve, as opposed to an image of what they are not trying to achieve.

232. DON'T think about pink elephants! – See above.

233. When teaching strokes that require speed to work, i.e. bow rudder or stern rudder or hanging draws, provide the speed at first by pushing the boat from the bank or pulling it with a throw line.

234. Strokes that require subtle blade control can be introduced by having the student hold the blade of the paddle, fingers on the back of the blade, whilst it's in the water. This aids in improving the student's awareness of the blade angle and subtle changes of angle.

235. To encourage an open paddling stance get your student to imagine the loom of the paddle smells very, very badly.

236. To encourage understanding of the blade position when teaching bow rudders the students can be encouraged to close their eyes and actively vary blade angle to achieve different results.

237. To help prevent 'slippery hand syndrome', use marker tapes on the loom to act as a gauge.

238. Use the draw stroke, at the bow, as a lead into bow rudders.

239. When bracing with a throw line, have your thumbs up, it's stronger.

240. Inspect rapids from river level.

241. Encourage students to pick their own line prior to running rapids to help encourage river reading skills.

242. Consider pairing your students to run longer, complex rapids. If the line is complex, pair them strong first and weaker second so they can follow a reliable line.

243. Always indicate the line to take, not the hazard.

244. Whether teaching 'seamanship' or 'river running' it is often a question of the coach bringing to a conscious level the things he or she no longer needs to think about.

245. When on the sea, keep 'a weather eye'. Keep looking upwind and towards where the clouds are coming from.

246. If you don't know what else to look for, keep an eye out for change. Whatever happens it won't catch you by surprise.

247. Surf wax on your seat gets your bottom to stick.

248. Surf wax on the cockpit rim gets your deck to stick.

249. Surf wax on your loom gets your hands to stick.

250. In flat hulled boats it is sometimes good to fit a sitting block to raise the paddler, this really helps performance.

251. A tow line or length of rope can be used to extend the keel line of a boat to greater directional stability. However it creates drag.

252. To help with breaking out, dropping the inside shoulder forwards into the eddy helps drop the edge and trim the boat forwards.

253. Breaking in is edge, breaking out is lean, (it's all to do with speed).

254. In a traditional canoe it is rarely ever lean, it's usually edge, achieved by shifting weight over a knee. (It's a speed thing).

255. In a minibus both emergency exits must be clear.

256. Use the jockey wheel on trailers.

257. In ferry glides allow the boat's angle against the flow to increase as you approach the eddy line, this allows the eddy to be penetrated.

258. Teach reverse ferries within the current, not from eddy to eddy, i.e. break in first and then reverse ferry. (That's how we use it).

259. As well as your spare clothes carry something to insulate from the ground.

260. The low brace break in is only used because people lose balance once the boat has slowed down, it's better to have people know how to balance the boat.

261. When choreographing a freestyle or surf run, remember that the most impressive runs have changes in height on the wave, changes in direction on the wave, obvious changes in speed on the wave and are fluent and controlled.

262. When helping people visualise a run, try getting them to visualise a run as a tube that changes size, direction and even colour for parts of the run.

263. Try surfing to music.

264. Finish your run when you want to.

265. When choreographing a run, leave moves with a high 'wash off' potential as an end move.

266. Read "The Art of Freestyle" ISBN 0953195635.

267. Questioning is a valuable but dangerous tool. Nothing demotivates someone like being asked a question they can't possibly answer.

268. If you fall into that trap a useful get out is to exclaim: "What a stupid question to ask!" This takes the pressure off the student and puts it back where it belongs ...on you.

269. Analogy is a coaching tool that only works with some people.

270. If your paddlers are trying to pull up on the paddle when they are trying to roll, you need to address the environment and the hip flexion, not the sweep.

271. Have a relaxed leadership style, that way when the going gets tough you can deal with it by being even more professional, rather than by simply raising your voice.

272. Always be honest with clients about judgement calls. If it's a gut feeling, admit it.

273. Sometimes clients are better off bailing out rather than trying to roll endless times; let them know when.

274. A white water roll should be a first time roll.

275. Teach a roll that comes from the lower back, not the back deck. Your students will thank you in the long run!

276. As the river gets harder the distances between breakouts should decrease, not increase.

277. When you are upside down you're not in control, the river is! That means in control of you and your group ...keep it to a minimum.

278. Whenever possible coach to develop the whole paddler not simply one aspect. Everything has to stay in context and in proportion.

279. Paddling is a case in point, i.e. the whole action is greater than the sum of its component parts.

280. The biggest block to teaching rolling is if someone has been poorly taught a back deck roll.

281. A Pawlata roll relies on a long lever and has a completely different body action to a screw roll. A screw roll is a lot more useful in that you don't need to waste time changing your hand-grip. People who are taught a pawlata find it very hard to learn the screw roll. So start with the screw roll.

282. Only teach a pawlata to people who really need the leverage (people who are too overweight and inflexible to learn a screw roll).

283. Overwriting ingrained habits is hard. Start off on the non-dominant side, it's less grooved in and easier to address. It also becomes living proof that the new skill is better and motivates the individual to practise the new skills on the dominant side.

284. Don't be afraid to say that it's based on your experience that an approach works, don't rely on research to prove the point. The science is too young!

Plas y Brenin Canoe Department

285. All the evidence says canoeing does not disturb fish.

286. Paddle with water in the river and you won't disturb spawning beds.

287. You have a 'higher duty of care' to your students.

288. Your duty of care is the same whether you get paid or not.

289. When you stop enjoying paddling stop coaching it!

290. Practise 'entryism'. If you don't like the system get in it to change it.

291. Professionalism is a bigger thing than simply being good in your boat!

292. Stay up to date.

293. Further training adds to your knowledge, it doesn't replace it. So all training is a good thing.

294. The sweep stroke in the low brace turn is a flat-water thing, it's not usually needed on moving water.

295. Teach people to set the angle of attack by using forward sweeps and by reverse ferries.

296. Bow rudders are moving water things. The blade is parallel to the boat but the boat crosses into the current at an angle.

297. Teach bow rudder in context, i.e. to break in and break out.

298. Beginners always put their decks on last, on top of everything and too low, explain how to wear the deck as well as how to use it!

299. When working with large groups, have some games that will help everyone to learn each other's names. A simple one is a game of catch where the person who catches the ball has to shout their name out before throwing it to someone else.

300. When teaching 'J' strokes to canoeists, remember that it's a small 'J' not a capital. This reduces the tendency for people to overcorrect and stall the boat, which happens because the correction becomes a reverse sweep.

301. When teaching 'J' strokes, remember that it's the pause at the correction phase that makes a greater effect, not a bigger 'J'.

302. When teaching tandem crews, remember that the strokes need to match, i.e. if the bow paddler is using strokes that rely on having forward speed the stern paddler needs to help provide it.

303. Watch out for people who think they are edging or leaning when all they've done is tilted their head to one side.

304. Find out what the psoas major and minor muscles do.

305. In a canoe, when fault spotting, think TASS - Trim, Angle, Speed, Stroke, in that order. Is the trim appropriate for the move? Is the angle appropriate, is the speed of the boat appropriate, and could a better stroke do the job?

306. River speed **+** Boat speed = lots of speed (i.e. paddling downstream).
River speed **-** Boat speed = no speed (i.e. paddling against the current).
River speed on its own = floating, with the scenery passing by!

307. Boat, get wet, boat, get wet, boat, get wet, sleep, wake up, boat, getwet, boat, get wet. Be careful not to overload with sleep and waking up.

308. On sunny days, when observing, wear sun glasses. When giving feedback, take them off.

309. NEVER wear mirror 'shades'!

310. Get your ears checked regularly!

311. Observation and analysis are foundation skills for a coach. It doesn't matter how well structured, tailored or timed your input is, if it's wrong!

312. Feedback on performance is not personal, it's observational.

313. To understand questioning as a coaching skill, watch Monty Python's Holy Grail. How do they work out that she's a witch?

314. To develop a positive mental attitude in preparation for when things go wrong in a serious situation, instil in your students the need to always finish the 'run' or exercise, even if they mess it up. They won't be able to give up in the middle of a 'gnarly' rapid or rock hop, so they shouldn't give up in training.

315. If you expect people to value training you should not be afraid of getting more training for yourself. If you truly believe in what you do you'll value it for yourself too!

316. When you are coaching or leading, 100% of your brain power is focused on the task. If on an assessment you are trying to second guess the assessor, you are bound to fail as only 50% of your brain power is focused where it should be. Concentrate on the task you have been set.

317. "Rules are for the guidance of the wise ...and the blind obedience of fools" - Anon

318. A good coach has good eyes, good ears and a small mouth (as opposed to a 'big mouth').

319. A coach's ultimate goal should be to do him or herself out of a job. If you teach paddlers how to learn, they will carry on learning even when you have nothing left to teach them.

Plas y Brenin Canoe Department
Notes

Also available
from
Pesda Press

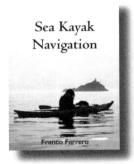

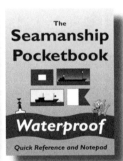

www.pesdapress.com